fotofax

WORLD WAR ONE:
1917

Philip J. Haythornthwaite

Front cover illustration: US troops arrive in Europe; see illustration 87.

Back cover illustrations:
Top: Cavalry respirators; see illustration 10.
Below: The effect of bombardment; see illustration 41.

WORLD WAR ONE:
1917

Philip J. Haythornthwaite

1. French infantry in a trench, a photograph which is interesting despite apparently having been posed for the photographer. The man at right uses a simple trench-periscope, and holds in his right hand a grenade with segmented casing (which split along the hollows to produce shrapnel) and apparently a 'striker' at one end; it is perhaps the *Grenade C. F.*, ignited by striking the projecting bar upon a solid object. The man with the periscope has two small metallic lace rank-bars on his lower sleeve, indicating a company officer (who wore one to three 35mm-long bars according to grade), rank-distinction being reduced to that size to avoid recognition by the enemy. Apparently he also wears the ordinary leather equipment, frequently another attempt to disguise rank from the enemy.

ARMS AND
ARMOUR

▲2

▲3

2. The French horizon-blue service uniform included a considerable number of variations: tunics appeared with both standing and turned-down collars, and the greatcoat (which could be worn as the principal garment in place of the tunic, unlike the employment of greatcoats in most other armies) was also produced in a number of styles, both double- and single-breasted, the latter originally designed for cavalry (with much longer skirts) but soon produced in infantry-length, with breast-pockets. Coloured collar-patches bearing the unit-

▼4

numeral were worn on both tunic and greatcoat, generally shaped to fit the edges of the collar, but variations occurred. (The number was normally embroidered in a contrasting colour: for engineers, for example, in scarlet on black). This young French soldier, the original identified only as 'Marcel' and dated 1917, has no collar-patch but a metal numeral instead.

3. Battlefield communications had not really kept pace with the advances in weapon technology, so that some failings of the higher command

resulted from an inability to alter plans quickly, according to circumstances, from the simple impossibility of contacting their troops. The field-telephone was the most advanced form of communication, though it was highly unreliable due to its land-lines which were vulnerable to enemy fire. This French telephonist sits in a folding, portable telephone-

booth; the crossed-cannon badge on his companion's helmet identifies them as artillerymen. The tunic collar-patch was scarlet, with the unit-numeral at the collar-opening and two chevrons at the opposite end of the patch, these details in medium-blue for field artillery, dark-blue for horse, and green for 'foot'.

4. At the beginning of the war, machine-guns were usually of the heavy variety, fitted on a tripod or wheeled carriage and requiring a crew of at least two. A major development during the war was the emergence of the more portable light machine-gun, capable of operation by a single gunner. Unlike many Allied forces, the French used the most famous of these, the Lewis gun, only in an aviation role; for army service one of the principal weapons was the 1907 Chauchat gun, modified to produce the Modèle 1915. It used the ordinary rifle cartridge and had a characteristic, 20-round, semi-circular drum magazine positioned beneath the barrel.

INTRODUCTION

Arms and Armour Press
A Cassell Imprint
Villiers House, 41–47 Strand,
London WC2N 5JE.

Distributed in the USA by Sterling
Publishing Co. Inc., 387 Park
Avenue South, New York, NY
10016-8810.

Distributed in Australia by
Capricorn Link (Australia) Pty. Ltd,
P.O. Box 665, Lane Cove, New
South Wales 2066.

British Library Cataloguing in
Publication Data
World War 1: 1917. – (Fotofax).
1. World War 1
I. Haythornthwaite, Philip J. (Philip
John) 1951–
II. Series
940.3
ISBN 1-85409-049-6

Designed and edited by DAG
Publications Ltd. Designed by
David Gibbons; edited by Michael
Boxall; layout by Anthony A.
Evans; typeset by Typesetters
(Birmingham) Ltd and Ronset
Typesetters Ltd; camerawork by
M&E; Reproductions, North
Fambridge, Essex; printed and
bound in Great Britain by The
Alden Press, Oxford.

After some 28 months of carnage on a scale never previously imagined, 1917 began with neither the Allies nor the Central Powers in a position of dominance; and as before, the successes of one side during the year were largely negated by events affecting the other. The revolution in Russia not only removed that country from the Allied war effort but also overturned one of Europe's oldest monarchies; and coupled with the near-collapse of the Italian military effort, and with horrendously costly but almost resultless Allied attacks on the Western Front which included a widespread mutiny among the French armies (which, providentially for the Allies, the Germans failed to exploit), this could have been decisive for the Central Powers. Their gains in 1917, however, were offset by the increasing exhaustion of their forces, major reverses inflicted upon Turkey in Palestine and Mesopotamia, and, most decisively, by the entry of the United States of America into the war on the side of the Allies. Despite President Woodrow Wilson's attempts to keep the USA uncommitted, unrestricted German submarine warfare and a report of prospective German–Mexican collaboration to attack the USA caused the immense economic resources of the United States to be committed against the Central Powers; although it would be many months before the American military would be deployed in substantial numbers, the boost to the prospects of the Allies was immense.

The year 1917 also saw the spread of the war to other nations. Portuguese troops were committed to the Western Front (with limited effect), the internal turmoil in Greece was resolved finally by the triumph of the Venezelist faction which brought that country into the Allied camp, and many other states followed the lead of the USA. Cuba declared war on Germany on the day after the USA had declared war, and was followed by Panama, Guatemala, Nicaragua, China (22 July), Siam (4 August) and Brazil (26 October, after the German sinking of a Brazilian vessel); Costa Rica, Haiti and Honduras followed in the next year, but none of these contributed substantially to the Allied war effort save in the denying of their ports to German vessels.

Tactically, 1917 witnessed a number of developments, including the use of heavy bombers for attacking civilian or industrial targets, the advent of massed attacks by armoured vehicles, and the so-called 'Huterian' tactic of rapid advances by-passing enemy strongpoints which were neutralized at a later stage. In the field of uniform and equipment, shortages of *matériel* still resulted in wide ranges of non-official items of dress, and there was an increasing use of formation- and unit-signs, factors which make even studio portrait photographs of great interest, as can be seen from some of those illustrated here.

As in previous *Fotofax* titles, the central data section concentrates upon one army: in this case the weapons, organization and insignia of the French forces.

▲5 ▼6

▲7

BOYAU
DE
TOUL

5. Among the more conventional 'trench artillery' were a number of French patterns which used the somewhat unlikely propellant of compressed air. The leading French designer, Edgar Brandt, in addition to producing the 'Type 90' trench-mortar, designed the 1916-pattern Brandt air-operated projector of 75mm calibre, with a characteristically shaped barrel which narrowed towards the muzzle. The Brandt was not the only compressed-air mortar employed by the French: others included the Boileau-Debladis *Obusier Pneumatique* ('pneumatic howitzer'). Range was determined both by the pressure of the compressed air and the angle at which the barrel was positioned; a maximum practicable range was about 300 yards.

6. Grenade-projectors were used by most of the main combatant nations, ranging from simple cup-dischargers attached to the muzzle of a rifle, to mortar-like weapons such as the German *Granatenwerfer*, which fired a grenade fitted with stabilizer-fins like a mortar-bomb or 'aerial torpedo'. Far less sophisticated is this French contraption for projecting rifle-grenades, which resembles a rifle on an elevating-frame, on a principal used for artillery during the sixteenth century. The cup-shaped discharger (or *tromblon*) on the end resembles that for projecting the 'Grenade VB' or 'Viven-Bessiere'. Note the grenade-shaped cloth badge on the upper sleeve of the attendant; such badges (usually in the 'arm-of-service' colour) were worn as 'trade' badges in the French army: this indicates a grenadier, whereas trench-mortar crews wore a badge in the shape of a mortar-bomb.

7. Shortages of equipment were endemic in all armies, resulting from the expansion of forces at a rate which outstripped *matériel*. The consequences were most marked in British service in the early part of the war, but shortages were felt throughout, affecting even that most prized symbol of regimental identity, the cap-badge: to conserve nickel, all-brass badges were produced from 1916, but some recruits could not even acquire these. This member of the King's Regiment (Liverpool) wears the leather 1914-pattern 'emergency'- issue belt instead of the authorized webbing pattern, and has an ordinary tunic-button in place of a cap-badge.

8. Some recruits of remarkably unmilitary appearance were swept into all armies, such as this studious-looking member of the Durham Light Infantry. This provides an excellent illustration of the 'soft cap', introduced from 1917 to replace the earlier, stiff service cap. The 'soft cap' had a stitched peak and band, clearly shown here, and could be folded up if necessary or even worn beneath the steel helmet. The shoulder-strap bears not only the metal unit-title but also the bugle-horn badge worn by light infantry regiments; fusilier regiments wore a grenade-badge in the same place.

9. As the war progressed, a greater proportion of young soldiers were conscripted into most armies. This portrait of a youthful member of Alexandra, Princess of Wales's Own Yorkshire Regiment (Green Howards) exhibits some interesting features of uniform, including the shapeless appearance of the 1917 'soft cap' with no stiffening wires to the crown and stitched peak and band; and note the use of collar badges, not usually worn upon service dress, in this case the cipher and coronet of Queen Alexandra after whom the regiment was named. The regimental cap-badge at this period was nicknamed (from its shape) 'the Eiffel Tower', the name no doubt resulting from service in France.

8▲　9▼

10. Attacks of poison gas could have an equally terrible effect upon animals as upon humans, so 'nosebag'-style respirators were designed to protect army horses. These British cavalrymen wear the later pattern of respirator, the so-called 'box' type, suspended around the neck in a rectangular bag made of webbing material, with a hose leading from the mouthpiece to the chemical canister in the bag. Although the British infantry generally wore the 1908-pattern web equipment except when it was in short supply, the cavalry retained the 1903-pattern leather ammunition-bandolier, with extra rounds carried in bandoliers around the horses' necks.

11. It was usual for gas-alarms to be positioned in every front-line trench. These varied from bells appropriated from civilian sources, hand-cranked sirens, shell-cases suspended on rope or wire to be struck like a gong when gas was detected, to simple wooden rattles. This French position is equipped with a klaxon-style alarm of a

12▲

type carried by motor vehicles; the man demonstrating its use wears the ordinary French tunic, an Adrian-pattern helmet bearing the star-within-crescent of North African troops, and carries the gas mask in a metal canister worn on a strap around the neck, here with the top of the canister open.

12. The German army's gas mask was issued in 1915, and was carried in a metal can slung around the neck; it was considerably more efficient than the early patterns used by the Allied nations. This German wears the ordinary cartridge-containers on the waist-belt (all leather equipment was ordered to be blackened from September 1915, though this only confirmed a practice already in vogue), and carries an old-pattern bayonet, the narrow-bladed 1898 pattern which was still used despite the issue of the wider, short-bladed 1902 and 1905 modifications.

13. In most armies, among the most-respected and often bravest participants were the military nurses who served near the front line; their role was

even more remarkable given the traditional place in society which women had occupied before the war. These French nurses, apparently leaving the entrance to a dugout, are equipped with gas masks and Adrian helmets, most unusual additions to their traditional costume; at the right is Mademoiselle Leladier, whose bravery was rewarded by the bestowal of the *Croix de Guerre*.

14. Many strange items of equipment were devised during the war, including this harness supporting a rope-handled cylinder to carry soup or stew from the mobile field-kitchens to the front-line trenches, in the hope that the contents would remain hot until they reached the line. The leather coat with fleece lining worn by this ration-carrier on the Western Front in the early weeks of 1917 would serve a dual role as insulation against the cold and against the heat of the soup-cylinder. Around the neck is worn the 'box' respirator, and the equipment demonstrates the continuing use even at this date of the 1914-pattern emergency leather issue.

13▲   14▼

15. The Vickers gun remained the British Army's principal machine-gun from shortly after the commencement of the First World War until well after 1945; justly famous for its reliability, it used a standard 0.303in. cartridge, could achieve a maximum range of 4,500 yards and a rate of fire up to 500 rounds per minute. This photograph shows a gun on its usual tripod mounting, with a crew whose shoulder-titles 'MMG' identify them as members of the Motor Machine Gun service. The Machine Gun Corps was formed in October 1915 and its Heavy Branch, formed in November 1916, became the Tank Corps in July 1917.

16. George H. Leishman of the Motor Machine Gun service; the Machine Gun Corps was formed when the requirement of machine-guns and crews outstripped those which could be accommodated by individual battalions, and henceforth were used in a role not unlike that of support artillery. Private Leishman wears the heavy greatcoat sometimes styled a 'British warm', leather gaiters (commonly used instead of puttees by motorized units) and a cap bearing the brass, crowned, crossed Vickers guns of the MGC with white-metal letters 'MMG' below, plus motoring goggles. A caption on the original records that Leishman was invalided from East Africa with fever in 1917.

17. Motor-cycle combinations armed with machine-guns would have been a most valuable reconnaissance or support force had the campaigning on the Western Front not settled by the end of 1914 into a static battle of opposing trench-lines. This section of the British Motor Machine Gun service was photographed in July 1917, and includes an interesting variety of equipment: most of the men wear short overcoats and 1908-pattern web equipment, and while most have the ordinary service cap, a few have removed the wire stiffening to produce the 'Gorblimey' style favoured by experienced campaigners.

18. A Belgian machine-gun section equipped with light cars with pneumatic tyres for the transport of the guns, drawn by dogs; the tradition of canine teams persisted in the Belgian Army. The crews wear the khaki Belgian service uniform, the greatcoats with a double row of five bronzed buttons and shoulder-straps with arm-of-service piping. Brown leather equipment including multiple cartridge-pouches on the waist-belt began to be introduced from 1915, and later British-manufactured web equipment, but these men retain the original Belgian black leather equipment with large cartridge-boxes and rectangular brass belt-plates. Their French Adrian helmets probably have the Belgian lion-mask on the front.

17▲

18▲   19▼

19. The staff uniform of the German Army is splendidly illustrated in this photograph of General Wilhelm Groener, who headed the munitions, supply and personnel branch of the War Ministry. The most distinctive feature is the staff collar-patch of gold embroidery upon scarlet backing, intended to resemble a loop of lace with tassel end, as worn in the eighteenth century. The field-grey cap had coloured band and piping and bore the universal national red/white/black cockade, plus that of the wearer's own State. The greatcoat has facing-coloured lapels (scarlet) and plaited gold and silver straps, which for general officers bore up to four silver stars (none for *Generalmajor* or major-general, one star for *Generalleutnant* or lieutenant-general, etc.) and crossed silver batons for *Generalfeldmarschall* (field marshal). The decoration at the neck is the *Pour le Mérite*.

20. Although the *Maschinengewehr 08* (machine-gun Model 1908) was a good weapon, its considerable weight and 'sledge' mounting made it less than ideal for trench warfare. The solution was the Model 08/15, introduced from 1915, basically the 1908 pattern with a shoulder-stock added, and a bipod mount instead of the 'sledge', producing a very much more mobile weapon. Its ammunition could be fed in by means of the usual belt, but to increase manoeuvrability further a 125-round drum magazine was devised. A lighter, air-cooled version was produced in 1918 (Model 08/18), but the cooling system was not very efficient and the weapon was prone to jamming. These two machine-gunners wear the tunics common in the German Army at this period of the war: the 1915 modification of the 1910 *Waffenrock* (left), and the 1915 *Bluse* with fly-front (right).

21. There was little opportunity for the employment of cavalry on the Western Front during the later stages of the war, though armies retained a mounted capability in reserve to exploit the breakthrough which was always desired but rarely achieved. These French troopers wear the mounted troops' version of the horizon-blue service uniform, like that of the infantry but with leather gaiters instead of puttees and a longer, single-breasted greatcoat with dark-blue collar-patches with numeral and two lines of braid in white, crimson, green and sky-blue respectively for dragoons, cuirassiers, *chasseurs à cheval* and hussars. Personal equipment was styled like that of the infantry; weapons included the 8mm carbine and the lance, usually of 1913 pattern.

22. The huge cavalry force with which Germany began the war could not be employed in the trench-war which succeeded the 'war of manoeuvre', so much of the cavalry was dismounted as the war progressed. Many units originally attached to infantry formations were retained in a mounted role for escort duty, but by the end of the war the remainder (about 80 per cent of the total) were grouped into dismounted units styled *Kavallerie-Schützen*, each of three battalions, each battalion

▲20   ▼21

based upon a mounted regiment and comprising four dismounted (infantry) squadrons (companies) and a machine-gun squadron; each squadron included a *Minenwerfer* unit. These cavalrymen are among those who remained mounted, with the 1916-pattern steel helmet replacing their original head-dress.

23. A British artillery battery 'dug-in'. The 18pdr field-gun might be described as the work-horse of the Royal Artillery, of 3.3in calibre with a range of 7,000 yards. It was capable of an effective rate of fire of eight rounds per minute, which explains the need for huge reserves of ammunition for a concentrated bombardment. The shells here are stacked in rows, laid alternatively nose-cap to base. Presuming that the pile of shells in the foreground includes one row shielded from the camera, this huge pile of ammunition represents less than ten minutes' fire for one gun at the optimum rate, which demonstrates the enormity of the quantity of munitions required.

24. The 'weight' of artillery increased as the war progressed, with guns of immense size being used to bombard enemy positions. The British 12in siege-howitzer, for example, needed a steel box filled with 20 *tons* of ballast to hold it in position after recoil. Only the static nature of trench warfare permitted such leviathans to be used: in more mobile warfare they would have been unable to keep up with the fighting, despite the enormous range of which some were capable (giants like the German 'Paris gun', for example, could throw a shell almost 75 miles). Naval artillery had been used increasingly on land over the previous century (most notably, perhaps, with the British naval brigades in the Boer War) and were again employed: this massive British naval gun on the Western Front is stabilized by a trail of enormous weight and by huge steel wheels.

22▲

23▲   24▼

▲25

▲26 ▼27

25. A major development of the war was the mechanization of army transport, which prior to 1914 had depended almost entirely upon horse-drawn vehicles. France pioneered the mechanization of artillery transport: the first four-wheel drive artillery tractor was constructed in 1910–11 by the automobile company Panhard & Levassor, and bore the title of 'Chatillon-Panhard', the former name from the Chatillon ordnance company for which the designer of the vehicle worked, Lieutenant-Colonel Deport. Although the French Army had experimented with lorry-drawn artillery from 1907, the Chatillon-Panhard was the first satisfactory off-road vehicle and at the outbreak of war the 50 such tractors in artillery service represented almost a quarter of the total mechanized transport of the French Army.

26. The German Army introduced a new range of ordnance in late 1916, from 7.7cm to 15cm calibre, initially styled the 'KiH' (*Kanone in Haubitzlafette*: 'gun on howitzer carriage'), and a modified design known as 'FK 16' (*Feld-Kanone* – field-gun – Model 1916). The gun illustrated (complete with limber which accommodated 24 rounds) was one of twelve overrun and captured at Feuchy, near Arras, on 9 April 1917 by an attack mounted by the 7/8th (Service) Battalion, King's Own Scottish Borderers, at a cost of 5 officers and 100 other ranks. This battalion was formed on 28 May 1916 by the amalgamation of the previous 7th and 8th Battalions, both raised in Berwick-upon-Tweed in September 1914, resulting in the somewhat unusual numbering '7/8th' of the combined battalion.

27. The personalization of artillery pieces with homely names was as old as the science of gunnery, and even led to such names becoming alternative generic terms, such as the 'Long Toms' of the Boer War. *Dicke Berta* (lit. thick or large Bertha), known

alliteratively as 'Big Bertha' to the British, was an immense variety of German siege-gun, the 42mm *Mörser*, designed originally to throw shells of sufficient force to penetrate the most modern of fortifications. The gigantic size of shell is illustrated here: note the crane needed to lift it into the breech of the gun.

28. Classed as auxiliary trench artillery was the *Albrecht Mörser* (mortar), a curiously constructed German weapon produced in three calibres, 25, 35, and 45cm. The barrel of this device was made of wood (the staves, as in a cask, ran the length of the barrel and are clearly visible here), bound with wire and reinforced by metal hoops. Manufacture was unsophisticated, even crude, and by the last year of the war the weapon was generally regarded as obsolescent. The elevating-mechanism is shown clearly: to absorb the shock of recoil it was equipped with a heavy base-plate like that of a more conventional trench-mortar.

29. The Hindenburg or Siegfried Line was one of the most heavily fortified systems of the period, with many defended positions of great strength, which caused the Allied attackers to suffer very heavy casualties. This is a typical 'pill-box' (named from its shape), basically a machine-gun position made of concrete around a framework of steel grids which stiffened the concrete to a most formidable degree, impervious to all but a direct hit by artillery or an audacious and hazardous infantry assault.

28▲ ▼29

30. A German 'assault detachment'. Groups of hand-picked men were formed for trench-assaults in 1916, when companies of *Sturmtruppen* ('stormtroops') were deployed at regimental level, each comprising an officer and three platoons of 40 men. By 1918 most formations on the Western Front had *Sturmbataillone*, each consisting of four *Sturmkompanie* plus a light trench-mortar platoon, flamethrower section, machine-gun company, headquarters and an artillery detachment with a 3.7cm gun. This unit is grouped around their 1908 machine-guns on the ordinary carriage, plus (left foreground) a 1908/15 gun with bipod mount. Most wear the fly-fronted 1915 *Bluse*, though at least one retains the 1910 *Waffenrock*; many have bags around the neck, fashioned from sandbags, to carry the hand-grenades which were one of the principal weapons of the stormtroops. Shorter carbines were popular, being less unwieldy than the long rifle for use in the confines of the trenches.

31. A trench gas-alarm made from a bell. The sentry, wearing his equipment over the greatcoat and with a fabric cover over the steel helmet, is a South African. The chalked inscription on the bell ('Duck Ye Nut') is a typically British piece of graffiti, exhibiting the humour which led to sign-boards such as 'Trench Mansions' being erected outside the filthiest and most decrepit of dugouts.

32. British troops receiving hot food from a camp-kettle or 'dixie', an oval iron pot in which stew, tea, soup and porridge could be boiled (but not necessarily simultaneously!); the flat lid could be used to fry corned beef or bacon, or make a variety of 'puddings', often the rock-hard army biscuit pounded into crumbs, bound with fat and mixed with dried fruit or jam to produce makeshift 'duff'. Stew was usually produced from 'bully beef' (corned beef) and tins of 'Maconochie' (vegetable stew in thin gravy), which with tinned jam (colloquially styled 'Tickler's' from the name of a manufacturer) and the hard

biscuit formed the staple diet. Like so much of the British Army's argot, the term 'dixie' came from India: from *degshai*, a cooking-pot.

33. British staff and infantry officers. This picture is most interesting because of the display of unit-insignia on the helmet of the officer at centre, an example of battalion- and formation-signs which proliferated in the later stages of the war; the position at the rear of the helmet, like similar badges on the back, below the collar, was to aid recognition by troops following. The Maltese Cross insignia is often associated with the Wiltshire Regiment (worn by the 1/4th Battalion in dark green, or red on the helmet), but was also used by the 1/7th Sherwood Foresters (dark green), 1/Rifle Brigade (yellow), 1/12th London (Rangers) (a slightly different shape, in black), and 70 Field Ambulance (orange-yellow), among others.

34. 'Tommies' entering the wrecked town of Péronne in March 1917. They wear the typical winter campaign uniform of the British Army: khaki greatcoats worn over the tunic (or a sleeveless leather jerkin instead of the greatcoat, as worn by the lance-corporal at right), with 'box'-type respirator in light khaki webbing bag slung around the neck and carried on the breast. The man second right carries the platoon's Lewis gun wrapped in canvas or sacking; the man in the background carries (doubtless with great care) the unmistakeable rum-jar.

32▲

33▲   34▼

35. Unlike the remainder of the French Army, the 'African' units of the colonial forces eventually were prescribed a mustard-khaki uniform of a shade not dissimilar from British khaki; this involved not only the indigenous troops but also the Foreign Legion, which was regarded as a 'colonial' corps. The complete issue of khaki was delayed so that it was probably not universal until the end of 1916, until when horizon-blue and khaki were worn together; the first Adrian helmets were issued in horizon-blue and re-painted later. This Moroccan *tirailleur* wears an unusual amount of camouflage and carries the original Lebel bayonet with hooked quillon, which was removed to produce the 1916 Lebel modification.

36. Although armoured warfare was not new in 1917 – British tanks had been deployed in the previous year – the action at Cambrai can probably be regarded as the first massed use of the arm. Developments in armoured warfare occurred rapidly: in addition to successive 'marks' of the original design, both France and Germany manufactured tanks, and a new variety of 'light tank' appeared, such as the British 'Whippet'. This vehicle, viewed from the rear and somewhat the worse for wear, retains the initial basic design but exhibits one of the first modifications, in the removal of the large steering-wheels from the tail.

37. German infantry stalking a British tank on the Western Front. The Germans are identified easily by the shape of their steel helmets; the man second from left is the operator of a 'Wex' *Flammenwerfer*, the most portable of the German flamethrowers, introduced in 1917 and easily distinguishable by its circular configuration with a gas-canister in the centre. Note also the 'unditching beam' fastened to the rear of the tank, intended to facilitate manoeuvring the vehicle clear if it became bogged-down.

38. Mud assumed a great importance in 1917, especially in the British offensive from Ypres, so that for the British 'Passchendaele' became synonymous with seas of shifting, glutinous mud. A typical problem is illustrated here on the Aisne front, with a French two-wheeled wagon bogged to its axle. The men endeavouring to free it carry carbines shorter than the Lebel rifle (as found especially handy for trench-service); note the cartridge-pouch carried at the rear of the waist-belt, and the fabric-covered, 1877-pattern canteen with its characteristic double spout, shown clearly on the central figure. All wear a

▲ 35

▲ 36 ▼ 37

rolled blanket, bandolier-fashion.

39. The popular concept of 'trenches' is very different from what actually existed in many cases: after bombardment and bad weather, trench-lines might resemble nothing more than scrapes in the earth or shell-holes sometimes connected by shallow gullies. This French position is not unusual. The *poilu* in the foreground wears a helmet with a dent which presumably demonstrates its efficacy as shrapnel-protection.

40. German officer prisoners of war with British escorts (left). The central figure, wearing his gas mask-canister slung over the shoulder, appears to wear the 1915 *Bluse* with the unplaited shoulder-cords of silver lace bearing the single star of *Oberleutnant*'s rank; *Leutnants* had no stars, *Hauptmann* (captain: *Rittmeister* in the cavalry) two. Field officers had plaited cords with none, one and two stars for *Major*, *Oberstleutnant* and *Oberst* respectively. Note the cuff-title 'Gibraltar', a battle-honour worn by units descended from the Hanoverian regiments which helped defend that place in the great siege of 1779–83, most ironically when serving under British command.

41. The effect of bombardment and soft terrain is shown by this photograph of a captured German position with a French

▲40

▲41 ▼42

soldier attempting to dig out of the mud a piece of German 'trench artillery' which has apparently been half-buried by collapsing earth. The weapon is a *Minenwerfer*, of 24.5 or 17cm calibre, both of which saw extensive use as close-support howitzers, achieving a maximum range of more than 1,500 yards. The name *Minenwerfer* (lit. 'bomb-thrower') led to the common British nickname 'Minnie' for such weapons.

42. The Polish army was formed in France from June 1917, its personnel transferring from French or Russian service, recruited from German or Austrian ex-prisoners of war, or from Polish volunteers from the USA. Being organized by the French, their uniform was of French style, plus the traditional Polish *czapka* cap (peaked for officers, cavalry and artillery) in the same horizon-blue as the remainder of the uniform, piped in the colour of the numeral and piping on the collar-patch: infantry (*chasseurs à pied*) green (plus a horn), artillery light-blue, engineers scarlet and the remainder white; the collar-patches were horizon-blue for infantry, scarlet for artillery, light-crimson for cavalry and black for engineers. These *chasseur* buglers wear the green horn-badge at the point of the collar-patch and apparently have the same insignia on the *czapka*.

43. Aviation services suffered terrible losses in action and from accident. The French hero Georges Guynemer was lost in 1917, being credited with 54 victories. Attending the commemorative parade at the field from which he made his last flight are two more highly decorated 'aces': Capitaine Heurtaux, supported on sticks, and René Fonck, probably the greatest of all fighter pilots, with 75 acknowledged victories (though his own estimate exceeded that number by more than 50). Heurtaux wears the original dark-blue uniform (often, as in British service, combined with items of uniform

from the individual's original regiment), while Fonck has the 1915 horizon-blue uniform: the aiguillette on his left shoulder is the *fouragère* (lanyard) of the *Croix de Guerre*.

44. A French decoration-parade at Noyon, about 70 miles north-east of Paris (overrun in the German offensive of 1918). The central figure, next to the French general in horizon-blue, is H. R. H. Prince Arthur of Connaught, who served as Extra ADC to the C-in-C, British Expeditionary Force (1914–17) and as a staff officer (GSO 2) 1917–18. Prince Arthur's appointment is indicated by his scarlet gorget-patches on the lapels (hence the nickname 'red-tabs' accorded to all staff officers), but otherwise wears the uniform of the regiment in which he was a major, the Royal Scots Greys, whose badge is shown clearly on his cap.

CHRONOLOGY: 1917

The strategy of the Allies for 1917 was decided towards the close of the previous year, at a conference at Chantilly convened by the French Marshal Joseph Joffre before his retirement on 31 December 1916. It was agreed that the main thrust for 1917 would be an Anglo-French push on the Western Front, concerted with Russian and Italian offensives. A secondary (though major) offensive was planned by Britain against the Turks in Palestine. Allied planning was complicated greatly by Joffre's retirement and the appointment in his stead of General Robert Nivelle, whose grandiose schemes clashed with those of the British commander, Douglas Haig. David Lloyd George, the recently appointed British Prime Minister, mistrusted Haig and thus settled the affair by placing the British forces under French command, which appalled Haig and the British Army. In contrast, and because Nivelle's pronouncements had revealed the planning of an offensive in the west, the Central Powers decided to adopt a defensive posture in both east and west, with their offensive manoeuvres limited to what they hoped would be a decisive drive against Italy.

Before serious operations commenced in 1917, a diplomatic development of crucial importance occurred: the entry of the USA into the war on the Allied side. Despite the efforts of President Woodrow Wilson to keep the USA neutral, the German proclamation of unrestricted U-boat warfare and the resulting destruction of US vessels, and the discovery of a plan for German support of a Mexican invasion of south-western United States in the event of US–German hostility, tipped the scales and led to a declaration of war by the USA upon Germany (6 April; war was not declared upon Austria until 7 December). The unpreparedness of the US military establishment, however, meant that although an American Expeditionary Force was planned for service on the Western Front, it was some considerable time before the vast resources of the United States could have a marked effect upon the war.

The Western Front

February–April: In accordance with their decision to defend on the Western Front, the Germans withdrew some twenty miles to a new, heavily fortified defensive position, the Hindenburg or Siegfried Line, which being shorter than the previous 'front' was easier to defend. The withdrawal was completed by 5 April.

9–15 April: As a preliminary to the Anglo-French 'Nivelle offensive', the British made progress in the Battle of Arras, including the capture of Vimy Ridge, but no breakthrough was achieved.

16–20 April: The 'Nivelle offensive' by more than a million French troops was a total failure, costing immense casualties and gaining hardly anything, proving that Nivelle's over-confident predictions were false.

April–May: After the carnage of the Nivelle offensive, wide-spread mutiny swept through the French armies; Nivelle was replaced by Henri Pétain, but for two weeks almost the whole of the French front was in a state of anarchy. Fortunately for the Allies, the unrest was quelled by Pétain before Ludendorff, the German commander on the Western Front, was able to exploit the situation.

7 June: After an intense bombardment, a British attack stormed Messines Ridge as a preliminary for Haig's major offensive on the Ypres salient, partly intended to break through the German lines towards the North Sea coast, and partly to divert German

attention from the French, who were still disorganized following the mutinies.

31 July–November: The Battle of Passchendaele (3rd Ypres). An immense British offensive gained about five miles of territory in three months' intense fighting, latterly in an utter quagmire resulting from prolonged heavy rain, wich caused the offensive to founder in a sea of mud. After suffering some 300,000 casualties, the British called off the offensive after the capture of Passchendaele village on 6 November.

20 November–3 December: Haig continued to pressure the German defences, still attempting to deflect German attention from the disorganized French, by an offensive which led to the first widespread deployment of tanks, at Cambrai. Great advances were made at the start of the attack, a genuine 'surprise' due to the lack of preliminary bombardment; but the Germans marshalled their reserves, counter-attacked, and with many of the tanks breaking down or being neutralized by artillery fire, the British made a partial withdrawal from their initial gains. Both sides had lost something under 50,000 casualties, but new tactics had been established: an offensive without a massive bombardment, and the use of armour as the primary striking-force.

The Eastern Front

March–May: The most climactic events of 1917 resulted in the collapse of one of the 'Great Powers' in the Russian Revolution. Triggered in part by the immense losses of the 'Brusilov offensive' of 1916, and based upon long-standing unrest, turbulence in Russia led to the abdication of the Tsar and the estblishment of a Provisional Government (12 March). This determined to continue the war against the Central Powers, but the influence of Bolshevik agitation (sponsored by Germany to destabilize the new government) undermined the authority of the military command, leading to the widespread murder of officers.

July: Despite the chaotic state of the Russian forces, the newly appointed war minister, Alexander Kerensky (head of the Provisional Government from 20 July), mounted an offensive in Galicia, commanded by Brusilov. The 'Kerensky offensive' initially made progress, but a German counter-attack from 19 July not only threw back the Russians but totally routed their now-demoralized forces.

September–October: A German offensive on the northern sector towards Riga had the same effect as that in Galicia: the Russian forces collapsed almost totally as their personnel deserted and fled. A new tactic named after the German General von Hutier was used in this operation, a rapid advance which by-passed strongpoints and left them to be neutralized by the German reserves, allowing for more rapid offensives. Faced with the complete disintegration of the army, the Kerensky administration fled from Petrograd to Moscow, and the Bolsheviks began to assume power.

7 November: The Bolsheviks, under Lenin and Trotsky, seized power and began to negotiate peace with Germany. (According to the Russian calendar, this occurred on 25 October 1917.)

15 December: an armistice was agreed at Brest Litovsk, ending hostilities on the Eastern Front. The total removal of Russia from the war allowed the Central Powers to concentrate henceforth on the Western Front.

The Balkan Front

January–11 June: Operations by the Anglo-French and Serbian

forces were inconclusive, co-operation between the Allied contingents was poor, and Greece was split with internal dissent between the factions wishing to support the Allies and those of King Constantine's party which favoured the Central Powers. Allied attacks at Monastir and Djoran (March) and in the Battle of the Vardar (5–19 May) made little progress.

12 June: Allied pressure finally caused the abdication of Constantine; his successor, King Alexander, re-appointed as Prime Minister the Allied sympathizer Eleutherios Venizelos.

27 June: Greece finally declared war on the Central Powers, thanks to the pro-Allied Venizelist faction. Although the Greek Army joined the Allied forces, no major progress was made before the end of the year, though in December the somewhat ineffective French commander-in-chief, Sarrail, was replaced by the more proficient Guillaumat, who began to institute a reorganization of the Allied forces.

The Italian Front

May–June: Despite fearing a major Austrian offensive with German assistance, after plans were made for French and British reinforcements if this should eventuate, the Italian commander Cadorna again launched an attack against the Austrian positions in the tenth Battle of the Isonzo. It had no more success than the previous nine.

August–September: Finally, the Italians broke through in the eleventh Battle of the Isonzo, making significant territorial gains and bringing the Austrian forces to the brink of collapse; Austria requested German assistance.

24 October–12 November: The arrival of considerable German forces enabled an Austro–German counter-attack in the Battle of Caporetto (twelfth Isonzo); using 'Huterian tactics' of by-passing strongpoints, the German spearhead smashed through the Italian lines, causing the total disintegration of many of the Italian formations. After a precipitate flight by much of the Italian Army, thanks to British and French support by mid-November Cadorna managed to construct a defence-line; but Caporetto was a colossal defeat, costing Italy more than 300,000 men (against 20,000 Austro-German casualties), and had the forces of the Central Powers been able to push on without outmarching their supports, the Italian defeat could have been total despite the sterling efforts of the Anglo-French reinforcement. It also cost Cadorna his command.

The Mesopotamian Front

22–23 February: Maude's Anglo-Indian advance continued its march to Baghdad, driving back the Turks at the Second Battle of Kut.

11 March: Baghdad fell to Maude's army.

27–28 September: As Turkish reinforcements were diverted to Palestine, Maude advanced up the Euphrates, threatening the Mosul oil-fields, and winning the Battle of Ramadi. In the midst of his triumph, Maude died of cholera (18 November). Contrasting with the reverses of the previous year, thanks to Maude's skill British progress in Mesopotamia in 1917 had been extremely successful.

The Palestine Front

January: With Lloyd George's encouragement, the British prepared to launch a major offensive in Palestine. At the Battle of Magruntein (8–9 January) the Turks were finally ejected from the Sinai.

March–April: Advancing on the Turkish positions between Beersheba and Gaza, the British were twice repelled at Gaza (First Battle, 26 March, Second, 17–19 April). The British commander, Sir Archibald Murray, was replaced by Sir Edmund Allenby, a general of very great ability in both tactics and leadership.

October: Having reorganized his forces, including a strong cavalry force, the Desert Mounted Corps, Allenby left a contingent to watch Gaza and attacked the Turks at Beersheba (31 October). Breaking through, he compelled them to retire from Gaza as well as from Beersheba.

November–December: Despite the arrival of the German General von Falkenhayn to revitalize the Turkish command, Allenby drove the Turks back upon Jerusalem, winning a significant victory at Junction Station (13–14 November). He attacked Jerusalem on 8 December; the Turks withdrew on the following day, and after a Turkish counter-attack was beaten off on 26 December, British possession of the city was assured. Allenby's brilliance had laid the foundation for total victory in the succeeding year.

The Turkish Fronts

In addition with Palestine and Mesopotamia, the Allies were in conflict with the Turks in the Caucasus and in Persia, but the turmoil of the Russian Revolution ended the former campaign totally, and planned Anglo-Russian co-operation in Persia was abandoned; both released Turkish resources for the more important Fronts.

As in previous years, 1917 ended with neither side in a position of dominance, though the gradual exhaustion of the main combatant nations was having an effect. For the Allies, the great successes in Palestine and Mesopotamia could not compensate disappointments on the Western Front, with only limited British gains at appalling cost, nor for the critical situation in Italy. Despite the Central Powers' major success in 1917, the elimination of Russia from the war, the entry of the United States offset the advantage gained, although it would be some considerable time before US resources could make much difference to the overall progress of the war. Both sides gathered themselves for a final effort in 1918.

FRENCH ARMY WEAPONS

The principal rifle of the French army was the Lebel pattern, which originated in 1886, designed under the aegis of the 'Commission for Repeating Weapons' established in 1883 to provide the French army with a new rifle. The work of a number of military weapons-specialists, its title 'Lebel' is somewhat curious, as the colonel whose name it bore (commandant of the Weapons School at Châlons-sur-Marne), though a member of the Commission, was less concerned with the design than were other members. The first small-bore military rifle to be adopted by any nation (8mm calibre), with a charge of smokeless powder, it was superbly produced and engineered so that its parts were interchangeable, facilitating mass-production. It was, however, probably too good, and retained far too long, being introduced into service at the very time when the superior Lee magazine was coming to prominence in other armies. The Lebel was an eight-shot repeater (a ninth could be loaded by actually placing it in the breech), but unlike the superior clip-loading weapons, the Lebel's cartridges (carried under the barrel) had to be loaded individually; thus in the time taken to discharge eight shots, it was only a limited improvement over a single-shot rifle and was thus virtually obsolete before it even came into universal use with the French forces, and remained inferior in rate-of-fire if not accuracy when compared with the weapons of the other major European powers. Minor adjustments to the original model were introduced in 1893, resulting in the official designation '1886 M.93'. It had an overall length (without bayonet) of 51.1 inches and a weight of 9lb 3½oz.

The Lebel was not the only rifle to be used by the French forces. Three patterns of shorter carbine existed, all of the Modèle 1890 specification and of similar design, with slightly differing weights: a Cavalry pattern, a Cuirassier pattern and a Gendarmerie pattern, with no bayonet save for the Gendarmerie; all used the Mannlicher-type three-round clip. Two patterns of Musketoon (Modèle 1892, for Artillery and Gendarmerie) were very similar, modified in 1916 to produce a new Artillery Musketoon with an enlarged clip for five rounds (Modèle 1916). Colonial troops (Indo-China units) were issued with the Modèle 1902 rifle, known as the 'Mannlicher-Berthier' system; these were the basis for successors to the Lebel which were used during the war, the Modèle 1907/15, with a clip of three rounds, and the Modèle 1916 with a five-round clip; though these did not supplant the Lebel throughout the army. In order to accommodate the clip, the magazine on the later models was sited beneath the breech, necessitating an increase in the depth of stock. The shorter carbines and musketoons were not restricted to those arms of service for which they had been designed: their reduced length was found to be especially useful in close-quarter trench-fighting.

The bayonet for the Lebel had a long, needle-like blade of cruciform section (sometimes styled an 'épée bayonet'), constructed for the thrust and thus having no cutting-edge; blade-length varied slightly (some broken bayonets were re-tipped and re-issued), but in general the blades were about 20½ inches. The hilt and locking-mechanism varied slightly according to the model of rifle to which it was issued, but usually had a grip of white-metal alloy (sometimes termed 'German silver'), though steel and brass grips were also produced; with a hooked quillon, which was removed to produce the 1916-pattern bayonet. The scabbard was steel, circular in cross-section, and with a steel button at the chape. This was not the only pattern to be used: musketoons and others were equipped with a more conventional 'knife' bayonet, with blade-length either 10 or 16 inches, with wooden or 'composition' grips (the latter a plastic-like material) and steel quillons.

Pistols were carried not only by officers but by other troops such as artillery and gendarmerie. The standard weapon was the Modèle 1892 revolver, of 8mm calibre, though the earlier patterns were also carried: the Modèle 1886 (similar to the 1892, also 8mm calibre), and even the Modèle 1874, of 11mm calibre. Automatic pistols were also used, such as the 7.65mm calibre Ruby, a nine-shot weapon very similar in appearance to the Browning.

Swords had little employment in the war, and were soon discarded; some, like those of the light cavalry, were still based on the 1822-pattern with brass hilt and triple-bar guard, while the 1880 modification of the Modèle 1854 cavalry sabre was common. Officers of all services officially carried swords, but these were rarely used on campaign, and almost never after 1914. Although the cavalry's firearm was by far the most effective of their weapons, three patterns of lance were in

service: that of 1823 (with triangular blade and ash shaft), that of 1890 (quadrangular blade, bamboo shaft, largely restricted to a training role) and the most prolific, the 1913 pattern (triangular blade and shaft of browned steel).

As in most armies, the French used a wide variety of hand-grenades, varying from home-made 'jam-tin bombs' to 'racket' grenades (a charge tied or wired to a wooden paddle shaped like a butter-pat or table-tennis bat), spherical grenades ignited by a friction fuze activated when the grenade was thrown, the fuze attached to a leather loop around the thrower's wrist, to more sophisticated patterns of the egg-shaped variety, with either smooth or segmented casing. The Grenade 'CF' Modèle 1916, shaped like a segmented egg-grenade with a lower projection, was ignited by striking the base upon a hard object, which depressed an internal plunger to ignite the fuze; the Modèle 1916 incendiary grenade, shaped like a tin can with a tube projecting from the base, was activated in the same manner. Others had the more usual ignition of a spring-loaded plunger held in position by a lever secured by a pin, such as the Modèle 1915 egg-grenade or the Modèle 1916 'Automatic' incendiary and smoke-grenade. Rifle-grenades were also used: the 'VB' (Viven-Bessiere) existed in the usual explosive version, and also a non-explosive variety for transmitting messages, contained within a jar-shaped head. These were fired from a cup (tromblon) attached to the muzzle of the rifle, propelled by a cartridge fired from the rifle, the fuze of the grenade being ignited by the bullet passing through the body of the grenade.

A number of patterns of machine-gun were used by the French forces. The Modèle 1900 Hotchkiss gun used a rigid brass ammunition-clip holding 24 or 30 8mm cartridges; the Modèle 1905 (Puteaux) and Modèle 1907 (St-Etienne), named from the arms factories which had designed them, used metal bands holding 25 cartridges. The St-Etienne, being air-cooled, was found to be especially useful in hot climates; and the Hotchkiss was modified to produce the Modèle 1914.

In addition to these conventional machine-guns, all of which used a variety of (generally tripod) mounts, the French used several light machine-guns or automatic rifles, though unlike many Allied forces only used the 1915 Lewis gun in an aviation role. The first of these was the 1907 Chauchat, named after its designer, which was modified to produce the Modèle 1915 CSRG. This weapon, using the standard 8mm rifle cartridge, had a simple mechanism and a 20-round semi-circular drum magazine positioned on the underside of the barrel; it was air-cooled with an aluminium radiator over the barrel, and had a flash-suppressor on the muzzle. Rate-of-fire was 240 rounds per minute. The next pattern was the Modèle 1908 or Berthier-Pacha, which had a magazine holding 20 to 30 rounds, placed under the stock; in some cases its shoulder-stock was replaced by a metal tube with a butt-plate. Rate of fire was about 450 rounds per minute; and like the Chauchat, it had a bipod mounting.

A lighter Hotchkiss machine-gun was developed in 1909, using a rigid band for 24 or 30 cartridges; its rate of fire was 650 rounds per minute, but its use was restricted to fortifications, tanks and aircraft. An automatic rifle of considerably limited use was the Modèle 1910 A-6 gun, utilizing a 7mm cartridge, but though designed in 1910 was not actually issued until late 1917, and manufacture soon ceased. A further automatic rifle was the Modèle 1917 or RSC gun, using the ordinary 8mm cartridge, actually adopted in 1916 but not produced in sufficient quantities for distribution until March

1917. It resembled an ordinary rifle (even to the provision of the Lebel bayonet) but had a magazine holding a clip of five rounds, accommodated in a projection beneath the barrel. An improved (shorter and lighter) version was styled the Modèle 1918.

FRENCH ARMY RANK MARKINGS

Although several variations of rank marking existed (for example, the amount of lace carried on the kepi of officers), the basic system of insignia was as follows:

Private 1st class (equating with lance-corporal): one rank-bar on cuff (for cavalry, one chevron).

Corporal (*caporal*, or *brigadier* in cavalry): two bars/chevrons on cuff.

Sergeant: one or two bars/chevrons of metallic lace on cuff.

Warrant officer: *adjutant*, metallic lace ring with red central stripe above cuff, the lace in the 'opposite' colour to the buttons (i.e., silver lace for units with yellow buttons and vice versa); *adjutant-chef*, as adjutant but lace of the button-colour.

2nd lieutenant: one metallic lace ring around top of cuff.

1st lieutenant: two rings.

Captain: three rings.

Field officer: four or five rings.

General of brigade: two silver stars above cuff.

General of division: three stars (cavalry generals also wore the stars on the helmet).

Marshal: seven silver stars above cuff.

From the adoption of the 'horizon-blue' uniform, rank-badges were reduced in size and the infantry-pattern bar was adopted by all; for officers, rank-bars could be worn on the front of the kepi and even on the steel helmet:

Private 1st class: one red rank-bar on the cuff.

Corporal: two red bars on cuff.

Sergeant: one or two metallic lace bars on cuff.

Warrant officer: one metallic lace bar with interwoven scarlet rectangles on cuff and kepi.

2nd lieutenant: one metallic lace bar on cuff and kepi.

1st lieutenant: two bars.

Captain: three bars.

Field officer: four or five bars.

General (more distinctions with increase in number of grades): two to six gilt metal stars above cuff.

Marshal: seven gilt stars above cuff.

In both systems of rank marking, warrant and commissioned officers wore lace rank-chevrons on their side-cap, the number of chevrons equating with the number of rings or later bars worn upon the sleeve.

FRENCH ARMY BADGES AND INSIGNIA

Badges affixed to the front of the *casque Adrian:* impressed in relief, often on an oval or circular disc, and often somewhat indistinct or crudely finished.

Top row, left to right:

1. France: infantry and cavalry; for gendarmerie, the grenade was often painted white.
2. France: artillery.
3. France: *Chasseurs à pied.*
4. France: North African troops.

Middle row, left to right:

5. France: colonial troops.
6. France: engineers.
7. France: unofficial style of rank-designation: two bars indicate lieutenant's rank.
8. Belgium.

Bottom row, left to right:

9. Russia.
10. Serbia.
11. Polish troops in France.
12. Roumania (cipher of Ferdinand I).

Other varieties included French medical services (rod of Aesculapius within a wreath of laurel (left) and oak (right)); Czechoslovak troops in France (letters 'SC' from April 1918, replaced by arms of Bohemia, Slovakia, Moravia and Silesia from July 1918); Greece (crowned shield bearing cross); and the US troops equipped with the Adrian helmet used the French infantry badge, but an unofficial US badge consisted of the national 'stars-and-stripes' shield within a laurel-wreath. French generals wore a number of stars on the front of the helmet to indicate their rank, often with the infantry grenade.

FRENCH ARMY FACING-COLOURS

With the adoption of the 'horizon-blue' uniform, arm-of-service distinguishing-colours were generally restricted to the collar-patch, which had piping and regimental numeral in a contrasting colour:

Cavalry: dark-blue patch, with piping and numeral crimson (cuirassiers), white (dragoons), green (*chasseurs à cheval*) or sky-blue (hussars).

Infantry: yellow patch with dark-blue piping and numeral; changed almost immediately to horizon-blue with dark-blue piping and number.

Chasseurs à pied: iron-grey patch with yellow piping and number.

Artillery: scarlet patch with bright-blue piping and numeral (field), dark-blue (horse), green (foot) or white (alpine).

Engineers: black patch with scarlet piping and numeral.

Train: green patch with scarlet piping, crimson numeral.

Medical service, administration, labour corps: crimson patch, grey-blue numeral.

Gendarmerie: black patch bearing white grenade.

French collar patches. *Top left:* the shape of the patch worn in 1914, colouring varying with arm-of-service. For infantry, for example, blue numerals on red; the 45th Regiment in 1914 served in the 8th Brigade, 4th Infantry Division, in II Corps of Lanrezac's Fifth Army. *Top right:* greatcoat and tunic collar-patch of the 'horizon-blue' uniform; for infantry, ultimately dark-blue numeral and braid on horizon-blue. *Bottom:* more usual shape of greatcoat collar-patch, coloured as before.

French officers' rank-marking is shown by this photograph of Ernest-Jacques Barbot (killed 10 May 1915) as colonel of the 159th Line Regiment (headquarters Briançon), which in 1914 formed part of the 88th Brigade of the 44th Infantry Divison. He wears the officers'-pattern black tunic with regimental numeral on the collar. Rank-distinction was carried on the kepi, which had a lace knot on the crown continuing as vertical lines of lace at the top of the sides of the cap: for subalterns these lines and knot were of a single strip of lace, for captains two and field officers three. One or two horizontal rings of lace encircled the sides of the cap for subalterns, three for captains, four for majors and (as here) five for colonels; lieutenant-colonels had five rings of which the innermost and outer rings were in the regimental lace-colour and the alternate rings in the contrasting 'metal', i.e., for a unit with gold lace (yellow buttons) the inner and outer rings were gold and the alternate ones silver.

FRENCH ARMY ORGANIZATION

Infantry Division

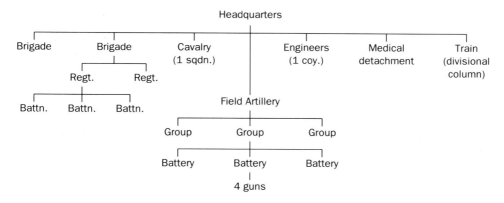

Headquarters

- Brigade
- Brigade
  - Regt.
    - Battn.
    - Battn.
    - Battn.
  - Regt.
- Cavalry (1 sqdn.)
- Field Artillery
  - Group
    - Battery
  - Group
    - Battery — 4 guns
  - Group
    - Battery
- Engineers (1 coy.)
- Medical detachment
- Train (divisional column)

Cavalry Division

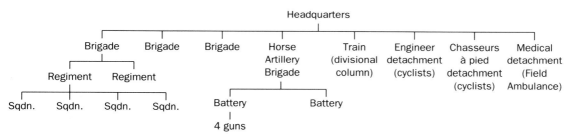

Headquarters

- Brigade
  - Regiment
    - Sqdn.
    - Sqdn.
  - Regiment
    - Sqdn.
    - Sqdn.
- Brigade
- Brigade
- Horse Artillery Brigade
  - Battery — 4 guns
  - Battery
- Train (divisional column)
- Engineer detachment (cyclists)
- Chasseurs à pied detachment (cyclists)
- Medical detachment (Field Ambulance)

Corps Organization

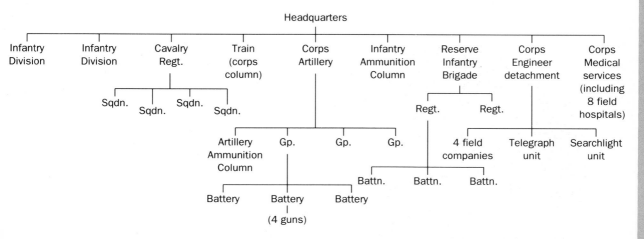

Headquarters

- Infantry Division
- Infantry Division
- Cavalry Regt.
  - Sqdn.
  - Sqdn.
  - Sqdn.
  - Sqdn.
- Train (corps column)
- Corps Artillery
  - Artillery Ammunition Column
  - Gp.
    - Battery
    - Battery — (4 guns)
    - Battery
  - Gp.
  - Gp.
- Infantry Ammunition Column
- Reserve Infantry Brigade
  - Regt.
    - Battn.
    - Battn.
    - Battn.
  - Regt.
- Corps Engineer detachment
  - 4 field companies
  - Telegraph unit
  - Searchlight unit
- Corps Medical services (including 8 field hospitals)

Note: the artillery and services (engineers, medical corps, etc.) noted above are those attached at Corps level: those attached at Divisional level were separate.

SOURCES AND BIBLIOGRAPHY

As noted in the previous titles of this series, much interesting material can be found in the illustrated periodicals of the time, for example the *Illustrated War News*, *War Illustrated* and *The Great War* among those published in Britain; but a comparison with earlier issues reveals a change in the selection of illustrations: those published in Allied countries now rarely depict 'enemy' subjects as they had earlier in the war, even though suitable illustrations were available, presumably, from neutral sources. Increasing censorship is evident in the later issues, with units frequently not identified and including what appears to be the occasional deliberate obliteration of cap-badges on pictures released for publication. As in previous titles, certain of the many 'campaign' histories applicable to the year in question are included below:

Barker, A. J. *The Neglected War: Mesopotamia 1914–18*, London 1967.

Bullock, D. L. *Allenby's War*, London 1988 (Palestine campaign).

Chappell, M. *British Battle Insignia 1914–18*, London 1986.

— *The Battle Soldier in the 20th Century*, Hatherleigh, series from 1987.

Fosten, D. S. V., and Marrion, R. J. *The British Army 1914–18*, London 1978.

— *The German Army 1914–18*, London 1978.

Gladden, N. *Ypres 1917*, London 1967 (personal account).

Hicks, J. E. *French Military Weapons*, New Milford, Connecticut, 1964.

Jones, I. *The Australian Light Horse*, Sydney 1987 (Palestine campaign).

Laffin, J. *Western Front 1916–17: the Price of Honour*, Sydney 1987.

Lawrence, T. E. *The Seven Pillars of Wisdom*, London 1935 (orig. 1926) (the Arab revolt).

Macdonald, L. *They Called It Passchendaele*, London 1978 (among the best studies of the period).

Macksey, K. *The Shadow of Vimy Ridge*, London 1965.

Mollo, A. *Army Uniforms of World War I*, Poole 1977 (the most outstanding work on the subject).

Nash, D. B. *German Infantry 1914–18*, Edgeware 1971.

— *Imperial German Army Handbook 1914–18*, London 1980.

Walter, A. (ed.). *Guns of the First World War*, London 1988 (reprint of the *Text Book of Small Arms*, 1909).

Williams, J. *Mutiny 1917*, London 1962 (the French Army mutinies of 1917).

Wilson, H. W. (ed.) *The Great War*, London 1917 (contemporary periodical, containing much significant photography and artwork).

Most useful for the campaigns of the whole war are the atlases:

Banks, A. *A Military Atlas of the First World War*, London 1975.

Gilbert, M. *First World War Atlas*, London 1970.

▼45

▼46

45. Even 'ordinary' photographs such as this group of three British soldiers can provide interesting information regarding the uniforms of the period. This group reputedly dates from 1917 (certainly no earlier than the previous year, as the sergeant-major (left) wears the ribbon of the Military Medal, instituted in March 1916 as a decoration for 'other ranks' one grade less than the Distinguished Conduct Medal); yet the seated man wears the shoulder-title of the Army Service Corps in woven cloth instead of the usual brass, the cloth title generally ceasing to be worn in 1907. The bar on the lower sleeve of the sergeant (right) indicates that he had been wounded.

46. Portugal remained committed to the Allied war effort even after the *coup d'état* of 9–12 December 1917 (the new president, Sidonio Paes, was assassinated on 15 December 1918). Here the Portuguese war minister, General Norton de Mattos (centre) is seen in London; much was made of Portugal's participation in the war and of their being Britain's traditional oldest ally, a connection reinforced by the close co-operation between British and Portuguese armies in the Peninsular War a century before: even the general's name reveals a British ancestor. His uniform is the national grey-blue similar to the French horizon-blue; officers could also wear a tunic with British style lapels, grey shirt and black tie, and another version had large side-pockets as worn by the officer at right. Generals' rank-badges were stars above the cuff; lower ranks had lace bars as at right.

47. Portuguese infantry in France in June 1917. The Portuguese service uniform comprised a single-breasted tunic with fly-front, trousers and puttees in light-grey-blue; a peaked cap of similar material was the usual wear, replaced here by the unique, fluted steel helmet of the Portuguese Army.

The two men at the end of the front rank are NCOs, identified by their blue shoulder-strap slides with silver lace bars (one to four according to rank). The light khaki web equipment is the Portuguese 1911 style, based on the British 1908 pattern, plus British respirators. The regulation arm was the 1904-pattern Mauser-Virguiero of .256in calibre (a carbine was also produced), but these men appear to carry British Lee-Enfields, adopted to facilitate ammunition-supply.

48. General Tamagnini, commander of the Portuguese Expeditionary Force. Officers wore a light-grey-blue tunic similar to that of the other ranks (here with four pockets: other ranks had only breast-pockets), with the usual light-grey-blue peaked cap, brown riding boots or (as here) ankle-boots and gaiters, and 'Sam Browne' belt. The rank-insignia of general was a silver star on the cap and three stars above the cuff. The somewhat unmilitary appearance of General Tamagnini and his ilk perhaps explains the somewhat derisory British nickname for the Portuguese troops, 'the Pork-and-Beans'!

49. The Canadian forces sent to Europe were not based initially upon existing units but comprised 'CEF' (Canadian Expeditionary Force) battalions, to which volunteers from civilian life and from the existing units were allocated; later whole battalions were organized by the pre-war regiments. Many of these CEF battalions were Scottish in composition and uniform, as shown in this photograph of Private Norman Rand of the 43rd Battalion, CEF (Cameron Highlanders), raised in Winnipeg. He wears the 'general service' brass maple leaf badge on the collar, but regimental insignia is carried on the sporran and on the blue glengarry: a rampant lion within a crowned strap bearing the battalion name and number, backed by a saltire and wreath of thistles and maple.

47▲

48▼

49▼

▲ 50

▲ 51

50. The insignia of the Canadian Expeditionary Force is illustrated in this photograph of William Irving of the 37th Battalion CEF (Toronto). The cap- and collar-badges are the Canadian 'general service' pattern (a brass maple leaf bearing a crown over a scroll inscribed 'Canada'), with brass battalion-insignia on the shoulder-straps, '37' over 'INF' (infantry). Note the Canadian-issue buttons (bearing a maple leaf within a crowned Garter, with 'Canada' above), and the standing collar rather than the more usual fold-down style.

51. Although it was more usual for New Zealand troops to wear the khaki slouch-hat with the crown punched up into a point (as ordered after Gallipoli), it could also be worn (as here) Australian-style, with the brim not folded up. Private Harry

Crozier wears the ordinary service uniform with the brass crowned fern-leaf badge enclosing the letters 'NZ', which served as the official insignia of the New Zealand Expeditionary Force, though his hat appears to bear a regimental badge. The waist-belt is from the 1908 web equipment.

52. Private William B. Perrin of the New Zealand Machine-Gun Corps, wearing the slouch hat in its familiar 'lemon-squeezer' style with crown punched up, and the unit badge: crowned, crossed Vickers guns with 'NZ' below, worn on the hat and collar; the brass shoulder-titles are 'NZMGC'. In British style the unit's companies wore identification-patches below the rear of the collar, of a star on a black square, the stars yellow, pink, green and red for 1st-4th companies respectively, a blue

star for headquarters, and a black star on red for the 5th company. The original of this photograph describes the subject as 'A Rum 'Un', a term which might be applied to other members of the splendid ANZAC forces!

53. Although Canada provided more Scottish units than any other nation save Scotland, overseas Scottish corps were not restricted to Canada. This picture shows Private James Edge of the South African Scottish (4th South African Infantry), raised in 1915 as the Scottish battalion of the South African Infantry Brigade for service on the Western Front. Shown here is the khaki kilt-apron (the button fastening its frontal pocket is visible), concealing the Murray of Athol tartan kilt (the 'government' or Black Watch set with a red

overstripe); the bonnet does not bear the regimental badge (a rampant lion upon a shield backed by a saltire and thistles with 'Mors Lucrum Mihi' on a scroll below) but the South African 'general service' badge, a springbok head within a wreath inscribed with the bilingual motto 'Union is Strength' and 'Eendracht Maakt Macht'.

54. The military medical services were supplemented by volunteer organizations, which in British and Empire service were usually referred to by the initials 'VAD' irrespective of their official appellation ('Voluntary Aid Detachment'). This Canadian ambulance-driver wears the cap-badge of the Canadian Red Cross Society, and has the insignia of a winged wheel with the initials 'VAD' on her lower sleeve.

54 ▼   52 ▲   55 ▼   53 ▲

55. Perhaps the most far-reaching result of the war was the collapse of imperial power in Russia, and the subsequent establishment of a Communist state; the Tsar abdicated and a Provisional Government was created in March 1917. Illustrated here is Grand Duke Michael, to whom the Tsar initially relinquished the throne; he wears the ordinary khaki tunic and breeches (cavalry officers were officially directed to wear green breeches, but in effect the khaki was almost universal), with the soft cloth shoulder-straps which replaced the more conspicuous, metallic-laced, rigid shoulder-boards during the war. Clearly shown here is the officers' version of the cap-cockade, domed and with a vandycked edge, in white, black and orange.

▲56   ▼57

56. Russian forces served on other fronts than the east: units were sent to Salonika and to the Western Front, and naval personnel had even supported the Dardanelles landing (the cruiser *Askold*, immortalized from its five funnels by its British nickname 'the packet of Woodbines'!) The abdication of the Tsar and the formation of the first democratic government marked the beginning of the end of Russian participation in the war: here, a priest administers the oath of allegiance to the new government to General Lokhvitsky and his staff of the Russian forces in France.

57. Alexander Kerensky (1881-1970) was originally war minister, and later head of the Provisional Government after the abdication of the Tsar. He attempted to maintain Russia's committment to the Allies, but the 'Kerensky Offensive' was not a success and his administration was overthrown by the Bolsheviks. In this photograph he wears a style of officers' tunic patterned on British lines, which came into use during the war, with pleated breast-pockets, large side-pockets and six metal or leather-covered buttons on the breast, something after the fashion of an English 'Norfolk jacket'.

58. Although internal unrest manifested itself in several of the combatant nations, it was nowhere so severe as in Russia, where fighting occurred between the rival factions. This is a scene in Petrograd: a street-barricade is fortified by artillery and over the wall of packing-cases there flies a red flag. Such scenes were only a precursor of years of civil war which followed the seizure of power by the Bolsheviks.

59. The war had an immense effect upon the role of women in European society, as the occupations normally filled by men passed to women when the men were called to the Colours; but although several armies included units of female personnel, they were employed mostly in medical or administrative duties. Not so in Russia, where a 'Battalion of Death' of ostensible combatants was formed. This illustrates the battalion commandant, Madame Botchkareva (seated, second from right) with her staff; the uniform is like that of the ordinary Russian troops, presenting an exceptionally unfeminine appearance.

60. In many instances, units of the Russian Army disintegrated totally in mid-1917, dissolving into fugitive mobs. Some remained loyal and attempted to cover the retreat of the fugitives, in which they were aided by the armoured cars of the British Royal Naval Air Service, led by Commander Oliver Locker Lampson. In this illustration members of the RNAS, recognizable by their khaki British uniform, aid loyal Russian troops attempting to stop the surge of deserters, one of whom (second right) is being threatened by the rifle of an RNAS officer (centre). The large barrel protruding over the loyal Russian's shoulder belongs to a Lewis gun carried by another RNAS man.

61. Italian infantry of the 'Lombardia' Brigade with their Colours; this brigade comprised the 73rd and 74th Infantry Regiments, with the distinctive white collar-patch with central light-blue stripe and white-metal five-pointed star at the front. These men wear the grey-green service uniform, including a wide variety of overcoats and Adrian-style helmet. New rank-badges were introduced from 1916, officers' insignia in the form of small, metal, five-pointed stars on the cuff, one, two or three for sub-lieutenants, lieutenants and captains respectively; and one to three stars on a patch bordered with metallic lace for majors, lieutenant-colonels and colonels. The colour-bearer has the single star of a sub-lieutenant; on his left is a lieutenant (two stars) and on his right a colonel (three stars within a lace border).

62. The Italian *Alpini* (mountain troops) were regarded as an élite formation and distinguished by grey-green felt Tyrolean-style hats bearing on the front an embroidered grey badge of an eagle atop a hunting-horn backed by crossed rifles, with a metal regimental numeral in the 'curl' of the horn. At the left side of the hat was a pompom coloured red, white, green, blue or yellow for the 1st-5th battalions of a regiment respectively, with a black crow-feather (eagle-feather for officers). Their green collar-patches or *mostrines* were flame-shaped and bore a white-metal star. This illustrates Italian NCO rank-insignia: a large (16mm wide) black chevron above the cuff with two 5mm chevrons above, indicating *caporale maggiore* (senior corporal); privates 1st class had just the large chevron, corporals one large and one narrow, and sergeants and *sergente maggiore* the same as corporals but in metallic lace.

63. An Italian sentry amid the Alpine snows. The Adrian steel helmet was first worn by the Italian Army in October 1915, imported from France, bearing French insignia and painted horizon-blue. From early 1916 they were supplied without badges and uncoloured, the Italians painting them grey-green. Later in the same year an Italian-manufactured helmet was produced, superior to the French original in having the skull and peaks made from a single piece of steel, with the comb soldered on instead of riveted, producing a much more robust item. Regimental insignia was sometimes painted on the front, and rank-markings on the left side, in black. This sentry, complete with leather and fur coat as a shield against the Alpine climate, wears his helmet back-to-front!

64. King Ludwig III of Bavaria meeting Austrian officers. From 1915 the Austrian Army began to replace its pike-grey uniform with one of field-grey, basically the same in cut but for a turn-down collar; German-style steel helmets (slightly modified in their Austrian manufacture) came into use at the same time, though were initially the preserve of storm-troops, the soft kepi remaining the standard head-dress. King Ludwig wears the *Pickelhaube* with a field-grey service cover; although it was withdrawn from the army's service uniform upon the issue of the steel helmet, it remained the semi-ceremonial head-dress and was still worn by staff officers.

62 ▲   63 ▲   64 ▼

▲ 65

65. A British dispatch-rider or 'Don R' in Italy. Despite Italy's being a European theatre of operations, the uniform of the British forces could take on a definite 'colonial' style: felt slouch hats and even topees were worn, with shorts, as here. The abbreviation 'Don R' was one of many resulting from the phonetic alphabet designed to improve the transmission of messages over telephone-lines: hence 'Ack Emma' (a.m.), 'Pip Emma' (p.m.), 'Ack-Ack' (anti-aircraft), 'O Pip' (observation post), etc.

66. Probably the most unusual member of the Serbian army was Flora Sandes, a middle-aged English gentlewoman who went to Serbia as a volunteer nurse but who progressed to a combat capacity, rising to the rank of sergeant-major, being wounded and receiving the Star of Karageorge (worn here on its red ribbon). In this photograph she wears Serbian uniform with the three four-pointed yellow metal stars of sergeant's rank on the shoulder-strap. Flora was promoted to lieutenant in 1918 and continued to live in Serbia after marrying a Russian officer, only returning to Britain after the Second World War.

67. The re-formed Serbian Army in Salonika was re-equipped by the Allies, their uniforms a mixture of British khaki and French horizon-blue. Like so many other nations, they adopted the *casque Adrian* like that worn by the French Army, but with the Serbian coat of arms (a crowned double-eagle with a shield bearing a cross upon its breast) applied in stamped metal on the front. This man at Salonika is equipped with the sky-rockets used for signalling.

68. A British trench-mortar on the Salonika front. The 'Tock Emma' (T/M) was a major development of the war, the best-known configuration being probably the Stokes pattern.

▼ 66

▼ 67

Although some types (such as the German *Minenwerfer*) had firing-mechanisms at the base of the tube, a common variety was 'drop-fired', i.e., the projectile was dropped down the tube and launched by a propellant charge ignited by a percussion cap in the base. The most familiar mortar-projectile was the 'bomb' resembling a finned shell (the fins to stabilize flight) but this variety, considerably prone to 'dudding' or failing to explode, was for obvious reasons known as a 'football' or 'toffee-apple' (from the rod which fitted down the barrel). The heavy base-plate absorbed the recoil. Note the variety of 'trench cap' worn by these men, with ear-flaps fastened over the top.

69. The Allied landings at Salonika had been frustrated by the unexpected declaration of Greek neutrality, and some internal conflict occurred between the Greek factions. On 12 June 1917 King Constantine was forced to abdicate and the appointment by his successor Alexander of the pro-Allied premier Eleutherios Venizelos resulted in Greece joining the Allies on 27 June. Before this, however, 'Venizelist' forces had been supporting the Allies. The Greek Army wore a khaki-green tunic, trousers and puttees (or gaiters) and brown leather equipment, and either a khaki peaked cap (replacing a kepi) or a khaki or light-blue side-cap. The standard arm was the 1903-pattern Mannlicher-Schoenauer rifle of 6.5mm calibre, and a similar carbine, modified slightly in 1914 to produce the Model 1903/14. The Venizelist forces (as here) were equipped largely by France and thus wore French-style accoutrements including the Adrian helmet with Greek arms on the front. The man at left foreground appears to carry anti-gas goggles around his left upper arm.

68▲ 69▼

70. The Central Powers in the Balkans: from left to right, Bulgarian, Austrian and German, at the station of Uskub, Macedonia. The Bulgarian wears a uniform of Russian influence; although a greyish-green service uniform had begun to be issued in 1908, earlier, brown uniforms and supplies provided by Germany were also utilized. The Austrian wears the national pike-grey uniform and kepi with the standard infantry waist-belt with two brown leather cartridge-pouches at each side of the buckle. The German wears the 1915 alteration of the 1910 *Waffenrock*, still with buttons visible on the breast but with turned-up cuffs, and with the tropical hat more usually associated with German

units in the African colonies. Khaki drill uniforms were also used by the Germans in Macedonia, Palestine and Bulgaria, not dissimilar from the ordinary uniform except for patch breast- and side-pockets, with either khaki caps with brown peaks, or brown cloth-covered topees.

71. Armoured cars might have exerted a greater influence than they did had not much of the campaigning degenerated into static trench-warfare. The value of such vehicles was proven in more mobile roles, in the Middle East and with the Russians. While the British Rolls-Royce cars were probably the best-known, many other varieties existed, notably (in British service) Lanchesters. This unit was photographed in North Africa, in operations against the Senussi rebels, who waged a sporadic war against the Allies over a considerable area around their Cyrenaica stronghold. With Turkish encouragement, the Senussi effort occupied the attention of perhaps in excess of 100,000 Allied troops (Italians, British and French in order of numbers) until at least mid-1917. Armoured cars performed most successful mobile operations against this enemy.

72. An anti-aircraft position in the Sinai. Although the slouch hat was not restricted to the Australian and New Zealand forces but was worn also by some British units, the tunics with pouch-pockets and waist-belts are typically Australian, the first pattern of drab serge, flannel or cord fading from its light khaki-drab dye to its original blue-grey colour. Legwear includes leather gaiters (left), puttees and shorts, the latter sometimes made by simply hacking off the lower leg of the trousers. The gun mounted on a post is the ubiquitous Lewis: the spotter (left) carries binoculars and the man wearing the service cap (with ear-flaps or neck-shade tied up over the top) carries a flare-pistol.

▲70

▲71   ▼72

73. Despite the increase of mechanization of army transport, horse-drawn vehicles remained vital assets, and in some theatres of war were more reliable than motor vehicles. This field ambulance, drawn up for inspection, formed part of the Allied forces in Palestine; the men wear slouch hats made famous by the ANZACs, but they were also worn by British units. Note the large red-cross flag affixed to the ambulance; and although the drivers do not appear to wear them, white brassards bearing a red cross are clearly visible on the left upper arms of the personnel drawn up on foot.

74. The 'Desert Mounted Corps' became famous for its actions in Palestine, but did not normally resort to mounts of this nature. This Worcestershire Yeoman, photographed probably in early 1917, poses for a typical 'tourist' image with pyramid and sphinx in the background. Note the lack of rank-badges on the sleeves: unlike the uniforms worn on the Western Front, officers' insignia on tropical dress was almost invariably carried on the shoulder-straps. The 1/1st Worcestershire Yeomanry landed in Egypt in April 1915, served at Suvla, and then with the 5th Mounted Brigade in the Imperial (later Australian) Mounted Division in Palestine until May 1918, when they became Corps cavalry of XX Corps.

▲75

75. A column of Turkish troops on the march, headed by a band of very mixed appearance. Although the Turkish forces wore a mixture of head-dress, including the Arab *burnous*, the fez or fur tarboosh (*kalpac*) was usually replaced on active service by the so-called 'Enver Pasha helmet' or *kabalak*, initially a loose turban but later stitched into shape to produce a cloth sun-helmet, further amended by arranging the folded cloth around a light, plaited straw framework, to produce a light but very effective sun-helmet.

76. A Turkish machine-gun company near Beersheba. Although the Turkish Army was armed and equipped in a predominantly German fashion, the cloth sun-helmet shown here was uniquely Turkish, owing little to European styles (though Enver Pasha, whose name it bore, reputedly based the idea upon the Italian topee); its great similarity to

the turban is shown clearly here. Note the boxes of ammunition (in belts) at the right of the central gun-team; the central man in the right-hand group is the observer, sighting and ranging upon the enemy.

77. Captain Oskar Teichman, the highly decorated medical officer of the Worcestershire Yeomanry (DSO, MC, *Croix de Guerre, Croce di Guerra*). This shows the typical service uniform worn in Palestine and Mesopotamia: resembling the ordinary uniform but in lighter-weight material and with rank-badges mounted on the shoulder-straps. The sun-helmet in this case has a quilted surface. Medical officers, though attached to regiments on an almost permanent basis, remained members of the Royal Army Medical Corps and wore the appropriate insignia, visible here as lapel-badges (a crowned

wreath with the rod of Aesculapius in the centre, bronzed for service uniform).

78. Many members of the Allied forces in Palestine found it a most moving experience to be campaigning in the Holy Land, around the places about which they had learned from infancy. This view of the Australian Light Horse on the road from Bethlehem to Jerusalem, but for the uniforms of the slouch-hatted ANZACs, might almost have occurred at any time over the previous two thousand years.

76▲

77▲ 78▼

▲79

79. A Mesopotamian scene: Turkish prisoners of war are bound and blindfolded before being escorted to the compounds established behind every front-line for the temporary accommodation of prisoners. Blindfolding was not generally used in the war, except in the cases of envoys who crossed to enemy lines under flags-of-truce, and who

▼80

would return to their own lines after their negotiations had been completed.

80. The uniform worn by the British forces in the Middle East (Palestine and Mesopotamia) was very similar to that used in India. This group wear a typical hot-weather campaign dress: shorts, puttees, shirt-sleeves instead of

the tunic, and topee, here with various additions in the form of additional sun-protection for the neck. Note the NCO chevrons worn on the shirts: rank badges were often attached very loosely to tropical uniforms to permit easy removal for the frequent washing of these garments.

81. Camel-transport had long been used by the British Army

in the Middle East and India. This scene from 'Mespot' (Mesopotamia) shows an Indian Army camel and 'driver' (the original photograph is annotated 'dispatch rider'!), with a British soldier in typical 'Mespot' tropical uniform: shirt-sleeves, shorts, puttees and topee, the latter with a quilted sun-shade added. This uniform was also worn in Palestine, frequently with the ordinary tunic instead of 'shirt-sleeve order'.

82. Methods of aircraft-detection were not sophisticated: whereas visual observers were sometimes provided with reclining chairs, this Indian soldier in Mesopotamia has no such luxuries, having what appears to be an extremely uncomfortable resting-place from which to use the large telescope which comprises his only equipment.

83. One of the most outstanding commanders of the war was Paul Emil von Lettow-Vorbeck (1870–1964), a veteran of the Boxer Rebellion and campaigns against the Hottentots. In 1914 he commanded in German East

Africa (Tanganyika) and though immensely outnumbered waged an aggressive guerrilla campaign with the greatest skill. In 1917 he was driven into Portuguese East Africa, but refused to submit and continued to fight (having marched into Northern Rhodesia) until after the armistice, only halting operations when the British convinced him that the war had ended. Here he wears the uniform of the German troops in the African colonies, field-grey (originally 'sand-grey' or khaki-yellow) with a grey felt hat, trimmed with the colony's facing-colour (cornflower-blue, poppy-red and white respectively for South-West Africa, Cameroons/Togoland and East Africa).

81▲   82▼   83▼

84. The campaigning in East Africa produced images which might have originated in the Boer War or on the North-West Frontier of India. This section of British infantry defending a blockhouse wear Indian-style uniform of light khaki tunic and shorts, puttees and topee, with 1908-pattern web equipment and, at least in the case of the man in the foreground, the 1907-pattern bayonet with hooked quillon which was generally removed in 1913. The bugler at the rear is an interesting relic of the old practice of conveying orders by bugle-call.

85. Operations in East Africa occupied large numbers of Allied forces and in many ways resembled an old-style 'colonial' campaign. Mechanization was introduced even here, however, for example this traction-engine hauling the British gun-boat *Mimi* across a bridge constructed for the purpose. Although the two British boats thus transported were established on Lake Tanganyika at the turn of 1915/16, hostilities continued until after the Armistice in Europe.

86. Although it took some considerable time for the physical presence of the United States' entry into the war to take effect, from the outset the boost to Allied morale was enormous. The first US troops arrived in France in late July 1917; by May 1918 there were more than half a million in France, and by late July more than double that number. This sentry wears the national field uniform of khaki tunic and breeches, puttees or leather or canvas leggings, and khaki felt hat with a cord around the crown in the arm-of-service colour (infantry light blue, cavalry yellow, artillery scarlet, etc.). The 1910-pattern web equipment was also khaki; the standard rifle was the Pattern 1903 Springfield of .30in calibre, but shortages of weapons led to the issue of adapted British P.14 rifles, styled by the Americans as the Model 1917 Enfield, also of .30in calibre.

87. Among the first drafts of United States troops to arrive in Europe was this engineer unit, seen here in London where they were received with rapture, a civic welcome and a parade past Buckingham Palace. They wear the US khaki service uniform, the Colour-bearers with leather gaiters and the others with canvas gaiters. The New Zealand-style felt campaign hat was not especially popular, and was replaced by the 'overseas cap', a peak-less side-cap; officers wore khaki peaked caps with light khaki band and brown peak and chinstrap, with bronze eagle badge. Steel helmets were not originally part of their equipment; these were issued in Europe, either the British pattern or the French Adrian helmet. Hat-cords for engineers (as here) were mixed scarlet and white, but officers of all branches wore cords of gold or gold and black.

85▲   86▲   87▼

▲ 88

▲ 89　▼ 90

respectively, and a silver eagle for colonel; 2nd lieutenants had no badges. The insignia was also worn on the 'overseas cap', and greatcoats bore black Austrian knots on the cuffs (brown for 2nd lieutenants), increasing in number with rank.

89. The year 1917 saw another terrible development to warfare: aircraft-bombardment of civilian and industrial targets, a far more significant innovation than the earlier Zeppelin raids. German 'Gotha' heavy bombers raided Britain and caused much consternation, presaging the events of 1939–45. This piece of burned-out fuselage belonged to a machine which fell in an attack on London on 6 December 1917; the man observing it wears the side-cap, 'maternity jacket' and greatcoat of the Royal Flying Corps (note the black shoulder-title bearing the unit-designation in white embroidery), while the sentry wears the brass royal coat of arms cap-badge authorized for local volunteer corps in 1916 but often ignored in favour of the retention of those units' badges. He carries the P.14 rifle, as issued to many such second-line formations, and wears the 1914 leather equipment.

90. This remarkable Heath Robinson-style device is a sound-detector, operating like a giant ear-trumpet to assist the detection of enemy aircraft. The German with his ear to the 'trumpet' demonstrates a late use of what appears to be the 1871-pattern bayonet with S-shaped quillon, which existed in two lengths plus a pioneer weapon with serrated back (*Pionierfaschinenmesser*). Note the woollen sword-knot (*Troddel*), the colour-combinations of which identified the owner's company.

91. Home-defence forces were formed by most nations. In Britain, these were generally styled 'Volunteer Training Corps' but initially were not part of HM Forces, officers were not commissioned and bore singular titles such as 'Platoon

88. A field-kitchen of some sophistication: an 'automobile cooker' of the US Army in France. In hot weather US troops could wear a khaki shirt instead of the tunic (with a light khaki tie for officers), and officers could also use a khaki-drill version of the ordinary tunic, of the same cut but with pointed cuffs. The men illustrated appear to have light khaki canvas gaiters instead of leather gaiters or puttees. Officers' rank-insignia was worn on the tunic shoulder-strap and shirt-collar, one or two silver bars for 1st lieutenant and captain, a gilt or silver leaf for major and lieutenant-colonel

Commander', and the force wore a grey-green uniform with unique rank-insignia and badges. From April 1916 their utility was recognized and they became part of the army under the title 'Volunteer Force', officers received ordinary ranks in September, but not until December 1916 were khaki uniforms introduced, and even then the older clothing and insignia remained in use for some considerable time. Here,

Commandant W. Bradley (seated, second right) and his officers of the Blackpool battalion are shown in the grey-green uniform, except Adjutant Shankland who wears the glengarry of the Argyll & Sutherland Highlanders, a tunic cut to resemble a Scottish doublet but with 'English' regular army rank-badges and (apparently) the cap-badge of the Blackpool battalion worn on the lapels, which with the khaki

kilt-apron produces an unusual uniform.

92. Prisoners of war on both sides retained their ordinary uniform, in this case with identifying numerals on large panels stitched to the tunic. This group of French, Russian and British prisoners was photographed by a German commercial photographer, Strauss of Cassel, at the Langensalza camp in June 1917.

Included are a corporal of the Hampshire Regiment (seated, second left) and a sergeant of the East Lancashire Regiment (seated right); the men wearing kepis are French and the remainder Russian, including one in Cossack dress (standing right) and an officer (seated, second right) with two-tone 'co-respondent' shoes!

The *Fotofax* series

A new range of pictorial studies of military subjects for the modeller, historian and enthusiast. Each title features a carefully-selected set of photographs plus a data section of facts and figures on the topic covered. With line drawings and detailed captioning, every volume represents a succinct and valuable study of the subject. New and forthcoming titles:

Warbirds
F-111 Aardvark
P-47 Thunderbolt
B-52 Stratofortress
Stuka!
Jaguar
US Strategic Air Power:
  Europe 1942–1945
Dornier Bombers
RAF in Germany

Vintage Aircraft
German Naval Air Service
Sopwith Camel
Fleet Air Arm, 1920–1939
German Bombers of WWI

Soldiers
World War One: 1914
World War One: 1915
World War One: 1916
Union Forces of the American
  Civil War
Confederate Forces of the
  American Civil War
Luftwaffe Uniforms
British Battledress 1945–1967
  (2 vols)

Warships
Japanese Battleships, 1897–
  1945
Escort Carriers of World War
  Two
German Battleships, 1897–
  1945
Soviet Navy at War, 1941–1945
US Navy in World War Two,
  1943–1944
US Navy, 1946–1980 (2 vols)
British Submarines of World
  War One

Military Vehicles
The Chieftain Tank
Soviet Mechanized Firepower
  Today
British Armoured Cars since
  1945
NATO Armoured Fighting
  Vehicles
The Road to Berlin
NATO Support Vehicles

The *Illustrated* series

The internationally successful range of photo albums devoted to current, recent and historic topics, compiled by leading authors and representing the best means of obtaining your own photo archive.

Warbirds
US Spyplanes
USAF Today
Strategic Bombers, 1945–1985
Air War over Germany
Mirage
US Naval and Marine Aircraft
  Today
USAAF in World War Two
B-17 Flying Fortress
Tornado
Junkers Bombers of World War
  Two
Argentine Air Forces in the
  Falklands Conflict
F-4 Phantom Vol II
Army Gunships in Vietnam
Soviet Air Power Today
F-105 Thunderchief
Fifty Classic Warbirds
Canberra and B-57
German Jets of World War Two

Vintage Warbirds
The Royal Flying Corps in
  World War One
German Army Air Service in
  World War One
RAF between the Wars
The Bristol Fighter
Fokker Fighters of World War
  One
Air War over Britain, 1914–
  1918
Nieuport Aircraft of World War
  One

Tanks
Israeli Tanks and Combat
  Vehicles
Operation Barbarossa
Afrika Korps
Self-Propelled Howitzers
British Army Combat Vehicles
  1945 to the Present
The Churchill Tank
US Mechanized Firepower
  Today
Hitler's Panzers
Panzer Armee Afrika
US Marine Tanks in World War
  Two

Warships
The Royal Navy in 1980s
The US Navy Today
NATO Navies of the 1980s
British Destroyers in World
  War Two
Nuclear Powered Submarines
Soviet Navy Today
British Destroyers in World
  War One
The World's Aircraft Carriers,
  1914–1945
The Russian Convoys, 1941–
  1945
The US Navy in World War
  Two
British Submarines in World
  War Two
British Cruisers in World War
  One
U-Boats of World War Two
Malta Convoys, 1940–1943

Uniforms
US Special Forces of World
  War Two
US Special Forces 1945 to the
  Present
The British Army in Northern
  Ireland
Israeli Defence Forces, 1948 to
  the Present
British Special Forces, 1945 to
  Present
US Army Uniforms Europe,
  1944–1945
The French Foreign Legion
Modern American Soldier
Israeli Elite Units
US Airborne Forces of World
  War Two
The Boer War
The Commandos World War
  Two to the Present
Victorian Colonial Wars

A catalogue listing these series and other Arms & Armour Press titles is available on request